Elizabeth M. Potter /
Beatrix Potter (contributor)

Beatrix Potter
Painting Book part 10

by
Elizabeth M. Potter

Content Page

Bibliografische Information der Deutschen Nationalbibliothek:
Die Deutsche Nationalbibliothek verzeichnet diese Publikation in der Deutschen
Nationalbibliografie; detaillierte bibliografische
Daten sind im Internet über http://dnb.dnb.de abrufbar.

Herstellung und Verlag: BoD – Books on Demand, Norderstedt

ISBN: 9783752866544

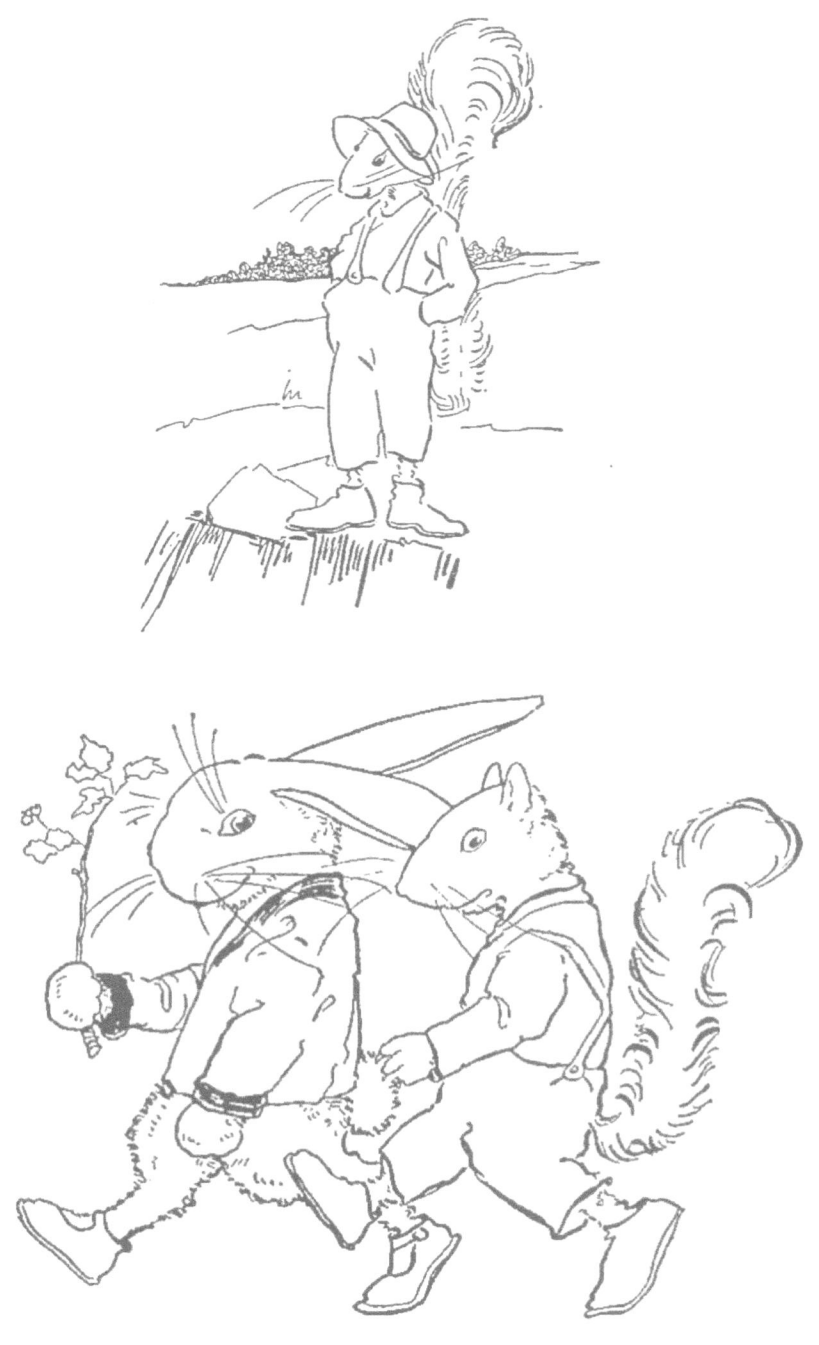

Further books of Elizabeth M. Potter

NOTEBOOKS
The Peter Rabbit Notebook
PAINTING BOOKS
Beatrix Potter Painting Book Part 1 (Peter Rabbit)
Beatrix Potter Painting Book Part 2 (Peter Rabbit)
Beatrix Potter Painting Book Part 3 (Peter Rabbit)
Beatrix Potter Painting Book Part 4 (Peter Rabbit)
Beatrix Potter Painting Book Part 5 (Peter Rabbit)
Beatrix Potter Painting Book Part 6 (Peter Rabbit)
Beatrix Potter Painting Book Part 7 (Peter Rabbit)
Beatrix Potter Painting Book Part 8 (Peter Rabbit)
Beatrix Potter Painting Book Part 9 (Peter Rabbit)
Beatrix Potter Painting Book Part 10 (Peter Rabbit)
Peter Rabbit Painting Book
CLIPART BOOKS
Beatrix Potter 99 Cliparts Book Part 1 (Peter Rabbit)
Beatrix Potter 99 Cliparts Book Part 2 (Peter Rabbit)
Beatrix Potter 99 Cliparts Book Part 3 (Peter Rabbit)
Beatrix Potter 99 Cliparts Book Part 4 (Peter Rabbit)
PASSWORD BOOKS
The Peter Rabbit Passw ortbook